Turn Your Customers into Profit

How to Turn Customer Service into Sales

Dario Cucci

Dario Cucci

Turn Your Customers into Profit

First Edition.

Find out how to get happier customers and more sales at
www.dariocucci.com

Table of Contents

Testimonials

"Good day, my name is Aaron Witnish, I have my business called Dz lifestyle and freedom. Dz has been operating for about two years now, and when I came across Dario, I was fortunate enough to get some of his time. He mentored me through my business, and the first thing he was able to do was to identify that I did not have a market, so it was quite hard to sell a product to people.

After that conversation, I was able to transform my business within the first few months by implementing the strategies Dario showed me, strategies which consisted of having a very definitive market, and adding val. After applying said strategies, I was able to increase my sales from the previous month by 100% percent.

On top of that, I was fortunate enough to get Dario to follow up with me on a more regular basis. Via his live training, I was able to increase my leads significantly and from those leads, I have been able to turn a lot more of them into real opportunities.

From there I was able to get two personal mentoring clients that are high-ticket items that save you quite a lot of money. Honestly, if you sit down and spend 20 to 30 minutes with

Dario, you walk away with a lot of valuable information that you'll be able to implement straight away. He does not take excuses, he is very direct, which is fantastic because you need someone who does not pull the wool over your eyes. He is going to make sure that you go out there and directly take action. I just want to thank you, Dario, because without your input and training, I would not be in the position I am right now. And I know that moving forward my business is only going to grow more from the value he has added to my life, the skills he has given me, and the ongoing support whenever , I needed any help.

Thank you, Dario, and I recommend your business and your skill set to anyone.

Cheers!"

- **Aaron Witnish**

"Dario is an excellent sales coach. By cooperating with him, I have in turn received impressive benefits. He assisted me in re-structuring some of my sales approaches and instilled confidence in a few domains I was struggling in. I would highly recommend Dario since he is creative, personable and employs a collaborative effort till one is satisfied with his/her results."

- **Deborah Jackson,** social media and marketing strategist, consultant, speaker, and author

"Dario Cucci has a knack for sales. It's in his blood! He has incredible profound knowledge and expertise to enhance your sales approach so that your franchise achieves fantastic figures that you perhaps never thought you could reach. Working with Dario will ensure he tailors your sales strategies to suit your franchise down to the finest detail. Missing out on that is surely not worth, as it will make a significant difference. Get in touch with Dario today and discover what's in it for YOU."

- **Deanna Roberts,** speaker, TV & radio presenter & interviewer, MC, photographer, and founder of The Princess Pursuit.

Foreword by John Spender

Note: As a guest author, I will release my chapter in his book, *Journey To Riches*, to talk about overcoming some of the challenges that I faced when I was at a low and struggling to recover from Bell's Palsy. So, I think it would be great to have that Foreword included.

When I first met Dario at an event in Brisbane in 2010, I knew that he was going to make a big impact in the world, I just didn't know in what capacity. I have watched his steady climb over a 6-year period and what impressed me the most is that he has achieved so much while maintaining his integrity. He has since gone on to help large companies around the world to improve their customer experience, and now he is sharing his knowledge with everybody – not just the corporate giants he consults.

And let me tell you that nobody knows the importance of building authentic, real customer relations than Dario. He has had to go through a lot to get where he is today, including a serve case of Bell's Palsy, though in true Dario style, he bounced back bigger than ever.

His book, *Turn Your Customers into Profit,* is a must read for any business no matter how big or small, and for anyone that is interested in becoming a better human being. The book is unique in its approach and filled with Dario's insightful wisdom. It's also not without its controversy, as Dario takes on heavy weights in the personal development arena, all for the greater good of you, the reader.

This isn't just a book that you'll read once, it's a book that you'll want to study and buy copies for your family and friends, as the principles contained in this book are worth knowing, inside and out.

With Gratitude,

John Spender

Who is This Book For?

If you are a business owner who must look after your customers to make sure that they stay satisfied while protecting the reputation of your business, then *Turn Your Customers Into Profit* is for you. If you are a sales person who lives and dies on commission, regardless of how many years of sales experience you have, this book is for you. No matter what role you play in a business, rest assured that there is something valuable waiting for you in this book.

In this book, I will walk you through many scenarios that sales people and business owners are undoubtedly familiar with. I will show you the importance of a positive mindset when speaking with a customer and how greatly it can influence the outcome. I'll tell you why you should NEVER use a sales script and how automation has killed our communication. I will walk you through – in great detail – how exactly you can turn an objection into a sale. Lastly, I'll tell you the simple trick to tripling your number of sales.

I recommend reading this book slowly and deliberately, drinking in every paragraph and marinating in the stories I tell and information I bring to you with an open hand. When you finish reading the book, be sure to keep it in your desk at work, or somewhere close by whenever you are interfacing with customers.

When it comes to the exercises at the end of each section, show no hesitation to complete all of them. Even if the reader believes that he or she will get nothing out of a particular exercise, you will never be able to succeed until you try, and the only failure comes in not trying.

Having worked with start-up companies as well as with small to medium sized businesses, I realized very quickly that the customer service, including the admin processes at the backend of the business, is flawed. In addition to that, sales people will do and say almost anything to get a sale.

Which brings me to the second point of this book – sales. If your sales consultant promises your customer something different than what they had previously been offered, or even if the customer misunderstands the sales consultant and buys a service that does not fulfil their needs, you are in big trouble.

The fact that you have terms and conditions in place to protect you from the customer taking advantage of your business does not help.

In fact, it hinders you quite a bit, creating a scenario in which you cannot make it up to your customers..

On top of that if administration departments such as marketing and accounting don't learn to more efficiently work together with the communication departments such as customer support or sales then a lot of the processes in place are flawed. This happens to be true more often than not from what I have observed and experienced over the last twenty years.

This book is for you if you are a business owner that is looking for some Inspiration, insight and practical Ideas on what can be improved within your business. There are some practical how to tips and exercises, however let's make one thing clear here this is not a "How to Book" as I want business owners to work *with* me if they have a business that needs help with sales and customer service strategies.

Why not make it a "How to Book"? Because there are plenty out there that do that, and I am a firm believer that every business has a different structure, including how they operate their admin, their customer service, and sales. To throw every business owner in the same bucket and give them as many as possible how-to exercises would devalue their business. That is not what my service is about.

When I work with the business owners I get fast results because I don't let them go through all the theory and studies of what should be done, before getting to the core issue what really need to happen and how we can get it done to fix the problems they have within their business.

An example of this is the marketing consultant I worked with "Deborah Jackson". When she came to me she had an existing Business that was doing well but it took her way too long to get new clients due to the process she had in place and the way she communicated with her potential new clients. After only one Skype session where I addressed how she could improve the process of getting new clients, I talked her through how to improve her sales strategy when talking to the prospect, and she could get the results she was after within 1 Week.

Before she worked with me she got one client a month with the old processes and Sales communication strategy she used.

After the very first Skype session with me, she then applied her new tactics. She got five new clients within one week. That is the result of me working individually and specifically with the business owners to get the results they are after by sharing with them the relevant experience they can apply to their business to gain momentum which is important. Now if you already have momentum in your business but you have a lot of complaints to handle then you will need different advice and training from me. I would then talk about how to improve the admin processes to make them more customer friendly whilst also looking at training your staff on how they can better engage with your customers to win the customers trust back and satisfy their needs.

To make a long story short, this book is for you if you are looking to gain some insight and inspiration with tips on how to improve your business by providing better customer care whilst also looking at improving your sales conversion and applying proven communication strategies in your business.

If for whatever reason you need more help with your business, then contact me at my website, www.dariocuccic.com, for your first individual 30 Minute Discovery Skype Coaching Call to discuss what you need is and how I can assist you within your business.

If I can make one request from you, the reader, that is to go to the website where you purchased this book and leave an honest review.

My Big Promise to You, the Reader

No matter how big or small your business is, I can promise you this:

Your productivity will increase by at least 20% while increasing your sales revenue by 300% or even more within the first 30 - 90 days of implementing these strategies. I can guarantee to assist you with my experience and knowledge to turn things around for the better with your customer service and sales communication strategy.

The reason why I am that confident in doing so is that I have applied the strategies and communication techniques myself over many years, continually honing my skills and have achieved excellent results with the companies that I have worked with in the past.

And I did so not only for one year but over fifteen years while having worked in Australia with self-development, financial education, and events companies before I moved back to Switzerland where I again applied those strategies to educate my clients.

One client, Axa Winterthur Filiale Kloten, applied a sales strategy that allowed him to visit his existing customers and get more than just one contract signed by the customer as he normally did. So, after he applied that strategy, instead of getting the customer to sign up for a new insurance contract, he ended up signing the customer for three additional insurance contracts, simply because of applying what I have taught him.

That's one of my most recent real life examples on the collaborative application of my customer experience and the results they are getting because of it.

When I work with you, I will be looking at all the things that you might not see, show you what needs improvement and then cooperate with you to make that happen as fast as you can apply it within your business.

My standard is to work with clients one on one only if they are committed to working with me for a minimum term of three months. The approach is key because depending on your size of the business; it will take time to change your non-productive habits and communication behaviors with your customers- a requisite approach to guarantee your firm's success.

Get started now and join my Fast Track to Sales Group Coaching and Mentoring Program for 30 days at the exclusive offer of just $47. Normally $495, this is my master program where I create personalized solutions to help you and your business increase sales and solidify relationships with customers. This offer is exclusive to those who purchased my book and will be removed after a certain amount of people take advantage of this deal, so if you're reading this, you're one of those lucky few. Sign up while there is still room left at www.dariocucci.com.

I hope you enjoy reading this book and use the strategies within as if they were your own. All I ask in return is that you take 90 seconds to write an honest review of this book so that others may also benefit from its contents.

PART ONE

Chapter 1 - The Million Dollar Sale Breakthrough

"You have to get up every morning and tell yourself, 'I can do this'."

One thing you need to know about me is that I have a talent when comes to making sales. Not only because I studied NLP, but because of the practice that I had when I had my franchise as a personal trainer for nearly 5 years.

I enjoyed working as a personal trainer, which contributed to my overall success in the business. After all, you must love what you do in order to succeed. When you're working a job that you despise, your clients will know it and your sales will suffer as a result.

Besides training my clients, my success as a personal trainer had a lot to do with how well I sold my services to get new clients and keep those clients of a long term basis. Had I not been able to both acquire new clients while keeping my existing ones, I would not have been able to pay my bills while building a personal training business.

One of the reasons I enjoyed selling my services as a personal trainer was because I knew the outcome of training my clients. I knew that what I did would transform their lives and improve their health. I always thought about the benefits of training my clients and how each session would positively impact their life. Each and every session had their own personalized program, created specifically to help them reach their fitness goals. My job was to help them go from being lazy and eating unhealthy to a cultivating a lifestyle that was more active. My job was to keep them on a regular schedule to improve their overall fitness, diet, and health.

In some ways, it was easy for me to sell my services because each and every client would experience a free trial training session before I made the sale. Every client knew exactly what they were getting with me – there was no pretense. If they enjoyed the free training session, they would pay for my services; if not, we would go our separate ways and I would move on to the next client.

After five years as a personal trainer, I decided that I wanted a career change. I got certified as an NLP Master Practitioner and started working as an NLP Life and Business Coach where I was assisting my clients to re-program their sub-conscious mind and let go of their limitations so that they could achieve their purpose in life with through proper goal setting.

Even after my career shift, I was still selling my services. As a life coach, just as I was while personal training, I would still offer my clients a free coaching session prior to signing them up. This method was so effective for me as a personal trainer that I implemented it in my life coaching business as well. As a result, 70% of the clients that took me up on the free trial session ended up becoming my paying clients. However, I soon realized that while I was making money with what I did, it wasn't enough money to do what I wanted in life. I needed to find a way to make more money than I did at the time.

Around this time, I got a call from one of the sales people working for Empowerment.

They were trying to sell me a ticket to attend *Unleash the Power Within, a new* Anthony Robbins event taking place later that year. I spoke with him at length and as we got talking, he got to know what I did for a living. Eventually, he offered me the opportunity to work for the same company. He was so impressed with my history and what I know that he thought I would be a great fit for their team to help them sell Anthony Robbins tickets.

So, he recommended me to his supervisor "Saira" after I sent in my CV. Then Saira called me to test me on the phone. During our conversation, she first got to know me a bit, then did a role play with me to see if I was a good fit. After we finished with the role play, she told me that I had the Job!

That's how I ended up working for a company called Empowerment and selling tickets to Anthony Robbins coaching events. The only catch was that I was working for a commission of the ticket sales. Although I was only making twenty percent of the tickets I sold over the phone, of course I had the benefit to attend *Unleash the Power Within* for free.

The only problem at the time was that I was not used to selling only on the phone. During the first two weeks while working with Empowerment, I had a hard time converting any conversation I had with potential customers into a sale. One of the reasons being was that the whole visual aspect of selling face to face was missing while I was selling over the phone. As studies show, this visual aspect makes up 65% of sales.

When we speak with people in person, they listen while having the added advantage of being able to see our behavior and body language. That 65% fell away when I started making phone calls to people to sell the Anthony Robbins tickets to *Unleash the Power Within.*

Needless to say, I was very frustrated at the time. I thought to myself, why can't I make any sales? I used to be so good before, what's happening to me?

I started to doubt myself and my ability to sell. I was also down to my last $300 in my bank account and no more money to cover my upcoming rent. The pressure to make a sale was big since without a big sale, I would end up falling behind on my rent.

During the first two weeks of making phone calls, I didn't just try to sell *Unleash the Power Within* of Anthony Robbins but also his other programs, such as *Date with Destiny,* which sold at $6,000.00. One of the previous customers that once attended *Unleash the Power Within* had a high level of interest in possibly coming along to the next *Date with Destiny* seminar, however, she was unsure after our conversation. The phone call I held the 4th day after I started working with Empowerment and it was a good conversation, but the customer did not confirm that she wanted to buy the ticket to attend *Date with Destiny.*

So, after two weeks of not having sold a single thing, I woke up the next morning and decided I will either make a sale today, or I will quit and look for a steadier job with a steadier income.

The Moment of Clarity

I went to the office and the first call that I made was to the customer that I had been speaking with about attending *Date with Destiny*. During our call, I had a moment of clarity. I realized that it's not about pushing someone into buying something, but getting them to understand the value of the purchase itself. The customer wanted to know what was in it for her, and it was my job to get her to feel secure enough so that she could make the informed decision. Making the actual sale was only the result of helping her understand how purchasing these tickets would benefit her life. After I answered all her questions I asked her, "Are you ready now to get the ticket and attend the next *Date with Destiny*?" she said "Yes, I am."

The customer paid over the phone with her credit card and I got the 20% commission. That one sale made me $1000.00, which at the time was enough to cover both my rent and enough food for the next month.

Once I stopped asking the question, "What's in it for me?" and started to see it from the customer's perspective, I felt like I could sell anything. Incidentally, my customers were also asking, "What's in it for me?" If I couldn't figure out how attending each event would benefit each individual customer, I knew I wouldn't make any sales. Just as I did as a personal trainer and as a life coach, I was helping people better themselves. I could quickly discern who wanted to attend what events and why – all because I was driven by benefitting the customer, not my wallet.

After that experience, I got a boost in confidence and my approach to selling on the phone completely changed, because I realized that I had to implement what I have learned from that for me to succeed. As a result of me applying what I have learned, I gained momentum and made a monthly average income of about $10,000 on commission alone. Within less than 12 months I made them over 1 million dollars' in additional sales. .

Best of all, I applied that strategy and honed it over the years I worked with other companies while selling their products and events on the phone. So, I always achieved 1 Million or more on additional sales revenue every 12 months regardless for which company I worked for or the setup they had with their administration.

The Sales Relationship System

This is why I call it "The Sales Relationship System", because every person I sold to was a customer that previously bought something before, then forgot about it. I ended up calling them, re-establishing a relationship, and building up their trust in the company and the products they sell, but also in me as a person. Because of that, I made a lot more sales than the other sales people I worked with since they were busy chasing down new customers to convert them into paying customers which takes a lot longer.

I also applied this strategy to people that never bought something but have subscribed to a list of the companies I worked for by downloading an E-Book or registering to order their free book.

Most companies that use internet marketing strategies are too lazy to implement the phone call strategy to get to know their customers, which results in them leaving a lot of money they could make on the table and losing those potential customers to their competition, which is a shame, because in all honesty, my belief is that it's worth getting to know your customer. Not through automation, but by actually holding a real conversation with them.

Do you recall a time when a conversation you had with a customer gave you a moment of clarity or epiphany which increased your ability to sale? Has a customer ever done or said something that had a significant impact on your life? What are some of the best and worst stories you have involving customers and customer service? I would love to hear from every reader out there and invite you to connect with me on social media @DarioCucci, or send me a message on my website, www.DarioCucci.com.

Chapter 2 – From 1 Client A Month to 5 Clients a Week

"Make the customer's problem your problem."

It's been said that a smart individual learns from their mistakes, but a truly wise person can learn simply from watching other's mistakes. Certainly, there is a learning curve when any sales person or business owner is just starting out, but by learning from the stories in this book, my stories and the stories of others, the time it takes to learn and implement customer service centric sales will be significantly lessened.

Aside from working for companies such as 21st Century Education, Empowerment, and Universal Events, I also worked with clients on a one-on-one basis doing Skype coaching calls where I would help them grow their business and increase conversions by focusing on interactions with individual customers.

One of the clients that I worked with was a marketing strategy consultant. When we first started working together, her biggest challenge was that she struggled to obtain new customers for her marketing consulting services. In fact, it took her an average of one to two months to get one new customer that paid her an average of $250 per hour.

Her problem was that the entire structure and process of how she went about looking for new clients was far too long winded. She had trouble asking potential clients to agree to her terms and finalizing the details for each and every offer.

This is what her process looked like when she first started her marketing consulting business:

1. First, establish trust through email marketing campaigns.

2. Then, call the potential customer to arrange a meeting.

3. Next, meet up with the prospect and discuss how she could assist them.

4. Then, after the meetup, send the prospect the outline of the work together with a quote.

5. After that, she would wait patiently for her prospective clients to respond to her outline.

6. If she got no response after a week or so, she would do a follow-up call with the prospective client.

7. If the prospect was unsure, she would then arrange a second meeting to handle any objections and get them on board.

8. If she still didn't get a confirmation after that, she would do another follow-up call to confirm that they are on board...

I don't know about you, but I was already getting a little frustrated just reading her SOP! (standard operating procedure). This is a very long winded process, and she was chasing down her prospects to convert them into paying customers for her services when what should be happening is the prospects are chasing her down with offer, practically begging her to work with them!

I asked her for an example of how she held discussions with her prospective clients in person or on the phone, and soon after listening to her pitch, I realized her problem right away. She wasn't selling the value of product to deliver to prospects. Also, she did not get the prospect to confirm their purchase. Instead she left it wide open.

To put it another way, her sales pitch was dead in the water. I was amazed that she was getting any business in the first place, because if I was her prospective client, I would turn around and run in the other direction. But, hey, if you pitch to enough people, eventually you're going to get someone who pays for your services out of pity.

I talked her through what needs to happen and instructed her on exactly what to say over the next 90 minutes. Then it was time for my favorite part of my coaching calls – we did a role play in which I get to be the stubborn, frugal, and unsatisfied customer and she had to try her best to make the sale.

When it comes to sales, role plays such as these are perfect for honing the cornerstone of customer service based sales skills. It prepares salespeople with a worst-case scenario in terms of a client you are trying to sell to, and in this case, the stubborn client will break character and give you advice from time to time. While that is definitely something you shouldn't expect when trying to make a sale with as real client – especially a "worst-case scenario" client – it prepared her for the worst and gave her the confidence to apply a new, communication-based sales strategy.

The final test is for her to call up all of the prospective clients who had all but refused her sales pitch. These were the ones that she had already given her weak pitch to and were basically too polite to tell her "no". One by one, she spoke with each of them with a newly refined confidence and sales strategy.

What happened during those next phone calls was no surprise to me, but for her, it was a modern day miracle. The following week, we got together to discuss the results of those conversations and how she was applying this new, customer service focused sales strategy. She practically broke down in tears.

"Dario, I won five new customers within the last seven days because of what you taught me." I could hear the emotion in her voice. Even over a Skype conversation, I could practically hear her beaming from the other side of the phone. "My average income increased from $250 to $750 an hour. Thank you so much for helping me with that."

Of course, I am very proud and happy that a client of mine has applied what I taught her and got such great results, which is why whenever I coach clients one on one in person or via Skype, I can pretty much guarantee that when they apply what I teach them, they will increase sales revenue by at least 300%, if not more.

Simplify Sales

The biggest obstacle that most business owners and even experienced sales professionals make is that they have a tendency of making each sale far too complicated. They just over analyze themselves and how they apply what they know, to the point where it ends up blocking them from getting the results they want. Because of this, sales people can often be their own worst enemy.

There is a saying that I love "K.I.S.S which stands for Keep It Simple Stupid" when it comes to sales and customer service. That rule applies too, if you want better results to grow your business while keeping your existing customers happy.

Whether you're the owner of a sales driven business, manage the sales department at your business, or if the customer service in your business needs a makeover, I will find a personalized solution for you and your business that is guaranteed to increase sales. Start by requesting a callback at www.dariocucci.com and together we will create a road map to sales success.

Chapter 3 – Why Existing Customers Buy More from You

"Effort and courage are not enough without purpose and direction."

You may have already heard the saying that "Existing customers are more likely to buy from you then when approaching a new customer." Well, it's much more than a saying – it's a proven fact.

A joint study by BIA/Kelsey and Manta found that existing customers not only spend on average 67% more than new customers during checkout, but retaining the business of an existing customer costs 10 times less than the cost of acquiring new customers.

The report concludes by noting that customer loyalty can bring big benefits to small businesses:

- Existing customers not only comprise a majority of top line revenue, but can dramatically affect a business' bottom line. According to the "Loyalty Effect", a 5% increase in customer retention can lead to a 25% to 100% increase in profit for the company.

- Existing customers that have an affinity with a brand are easier to up-sell and cross-sell. They already know and like what a brand does, so there is a measure of trust not afforded to an unknown company.

- Repeat customers are more likely to refer their friends and family to a business via word-of-mouth, online reviews, and social sites. Technology has amplified the reach of customers, making it easier to share recommendations about a particular business.

Once businesses truly grasp the impact their customer base has on their long term business viability, they can spend more of their time and budget focused on existing customers, which not only saves them money – it makes for explosive revenue growth.

Because of this, it puzzles me that so many small businesses and even large corporations spend their time and resources it takes to chase down and win over new customers instead of simply looking after their existing ones.

Old vs New Sales Strategies

The old thinking is that no matter how many customers one has, there is always room for more new customers, no matter what the price. While this idea was certainly true about 10 to 20 years ago, all of that has changed.

One reason is that, in today's world of distant social media friendships and fully automated businesses, people have come to value authentic personal connection more than anything.

Customers often feel like they are being treated like a number because of all the automation that has now been implemented by businesses around the world. They call customer support with one simple question only to be forced to navigate through a complex series of automated messages, leaving a customer feeling frustrated, isolated, and more often than not, they still don't have the answer to the one question the called about.

When a business makes it their mission to do something that truly benefits their customers, it makes all the difference. These simple things, like finding the best product or service that is the right fit for each individual customer instead of starting with your most expensive products or always upselling, is what drives repeat business.

When you start to view your customers as your friends, your neighbors, as human beings just like you instead of seeing them as just another source of revenue on your way to filling a quota – then you'll find that the revenue comes freely and frequently. When you stop looking at quotas and start looking at the level of satisfaction of your customers, you'll start to double or triple your income.

When your customers realize that you are the only business in your industry that is dedicated to actually helping them solve their problems with your products or services – that's when you create customers who are loyal to your brand – the perfect customer.

Chapter 4 – Why Sales Aren't a Number Game

"Motivation is what gets you started. Habit is what keeps you going."

Have you ever heard the saying, "Sales is a numbers game"? If you've ever worked in sales, you have undoubtedly heard that saying at least once (or if you worked at a cold call center, once every hour of the work day). But sales isn't supposed to be a numbers game. This archaic mentality is what will lead you to spending a whole lot of time and energy trying to convert the unconvertible.

I don't know who came up with that saying, but they are dead wrong – and here is why. It is incredibly short sighted to think that sales are a simply game of asking as many people as possible for money, then hoping and praying that eventually someone will cave in and fork over their cash. Having worked in a variety of different industries, I've witnessed firsthand that regardless of what industry you work in, the one common denominator that all salespeople should consider is that customers are people – human beings just like you and I – and that they are certainly not numbers to be checked off one-by-one.

The bottom line is that businesses treat their customers as numbers. That is a fact which is one of the biggest problems we have in the world of business today. If the customer were just a number, you would not need to care how they feel, think or talk about your product or service after they bought it. Instead, you would just keep on making money from them without looking after your existing customers.

They Are a People Game

Some businesses offer subscription services, such as mobile phones, online memberships, hosting, and many other products. As a result, they lose their customers within their first 12 months and get bad reviews on customer care, support and even their products. Many companies use ads and marketing strategies to win new customers, then, as soon as they have them, they no longer care about looking after them or following up. It's as if once the money is in their hands, the customer ceases to exist.

This unsympathetic approach to customer service can often turn fatal for businesses of any size. As a result of their poor customer care and support systems in place, businesses end up losing their customers just as fast as they got them.

Which brings me to the point: that sales aren't a numbers game, but a people game. When you have a great relationship with your customers they will always come back to buy more from you, not to mention send more customer referrals your way. The sales revenue, the numbers in your account, and even the success of your business are just a few of the many results of you selling your product. The thing that matters most is to look after your existing customers to the best of your abilities. This will not only increase your sales, but also improve your public reputation as a company, which is very important these days in regards to building a long lasting, successful business.

Even before a product can hit the shelves – or even before it's available in online stores – there are hundreds of hours of market research that takes place. Research on what type of consumer your demographic is made up of, customers like, what is in demand, what customers need, what they do not like about competing products, where do they currently spend their money, and on what?

From the beginning of developing a product or offering a service, all the way up until it is actually sold and starts to generate revenue, and even throughout the entire sales process, every single aspect shapes a product or service revolves around the actual customers that are buying what you're selling.

In today's market, businesses who believe that sales are a numbers game are setting themselves up for failure. Sales is now – and always has been – a people game. It's a game of winning their trust before they even consider buying from you, a game of demonstrating the value of not just what you're selling to them, but that you and your sales pitch are valuable enough to take up their time.

You can hire the best product development team to come out with the most effective, aesthetically pleasing, and indestructible product on the planet – but if customers don't trust the person selling it, they won't buy it.

At the end of the day, all you need to remember is to treat people like people, not a paycheck.

Breaking Down a Sale

Now, let's take a closer look at what happens during a sale.

In order for a customer to buy a product, the person selling that product needs to make a conversion. You hear the word "conversion" tossed around a lot in sales, but what that actually means is that you are converting a non-customer into a customer. Not only is that a crucial part of any business actually making money through selling their products, but a conversion is the beginning of a beautiful relationship with a business and a consumer.

How sales people actually make the conversion varies greatly depending on the medium. For example, sales people who try to make a conversion over the phone are at a severe disadvantage compared to sales people who have their customers inside their store, where they can physically show them a product. When selling products in person, this visual aspect plays a key role in purchasing decisions. A phone sales person is tasked with the job of bringing each prospective customer through the sales process of creating value, building a relationship, and so forth – all during a short phone conversation!

The formula for internet sales conversions is a bit trickier and can get extremely complicated. One of the most common methods that businesses use to make conversions over the internet is through a one way presentation or sales video, although there are virtually an infinite amount of internet marketing tactics to increase conversions, paid advertising is still the leading choice for businesses operating on the web. Digital advertising revenue reached an all-time high in 2015 at nearly $60 billion – and it's only going up.

(Source: Marketing Land, http://marketingland.com/us-digital-ad-revenues-60-billion-2015-iab-174043)

What all three of these sales people have in common is that, regardless of where the sale is taking place, they need to convince the customer that what they are selling is valuable. Thus, whoever is doing the selling needs to be extremely knowledgeable about every aspect of the product, regardless of from where they are doing the selling. When a sales person has no trouble explaining every little detail of the product that they're selling to the customer, the customer also feels informed and more confident in their purchasing decision. This also influences a customer's level of trust the company or person doing the selling.

As we can see, every sales person needs to first understand the value of the product themselves before they can convince customers that they will benefit from purchasing the product.

Dario Cucci

In the end, both sales people and businesses who understand that "making sales are a people game" are the ones who end up with the bigger numbers.

Part One Summary & Action Items

- When you cease to focus on making the sale, you will start to make more and more sales.

- Building relationships with your customers, rather than the sale itself, will allow you to increase your sales over a long period of time.

Action Items:

1. The next time you make a phone call to a customer, don't look at the time.

   Implementation Tip: When you get to the office, be sure to take off your watch and put it in a drawer. Get in the habit of not checking your phone to see what time it is. Once you begin to build that habit, you have no problem having conversations with customers without keeping an eye on the time.

2. Get out of your comfort zone and ask personal questions about the customer. Learn about their hobbies, family, past times, and passions.

   Implementation Tip: A good way to break the ice and dig a little deeper is to ask your customer if they have kids or are married. Find common ground with your customer. Ask them if they follow a certain sports team or even something as simple as what they did over the weekend.

3. Take time to learn about your customer and their specific wants and needs.

   Implementation Tip: Ask your customer what their short and long term goals are, what inspires them, and what value they see in your product or service.

4. Observe the difference between your previous phone calls to customers and your customer service centric phone calls. How did you feel during either?

   Implementation Tip: Take 5 minutes to clear your head and ground yourself by sitting in a quiet place and focusing on your deep breathing. When you're ready, grab a pen and paper and write out how your last phone call made you feel.

PART TWO

Chapter 5 – Your Mindset Matters to Make a Sale

"Attitude is a little thing that makes a big difference."

Most business owners and managers of companies play favorites with their sales department more so than any other part of their business. After all, that's where all of the money is being made.

Incidentally, the sales department is also one of the most stressful jobs at any company. Specifically, people who work in the sales department, companies report up to five times higher stress levels than any other position. That's because it's one of the few roles in a company where you are under constant pressure to perform. Everyone in the company wants to see bigger and better sales numbers from you - in fact, businesses depend on it - and if you're a sales person who can't make a sale, you'll quickly find yourself on the street looking for a new job.

Sales are also highly stressful from the perspective of business owners. If you want to expand your business and if there is a lack of cash flow happening because of the limited amount of sales that are being made, you are being held back by your own sales department. Your business can't grow the way you want it to with the wrong sales people who are using outdated sales strategies.

I understand why the pressure is so high when it comes to working in the sales department, office or call center where you have to make sales happen over the phone, or set up meetings to make the conversion happen face-to-face. After all, sales are at the heart of any thriving enterprise.

That's why it is so important that each person who works in sales, as well as every business owner who sells his or her own products and services, to learn how to not let the stress of making the sale affect them negatively. Instead, a massive shift needs to take place when it comes to their state of mind, emotions and body when making sales.

If one does not learn how to do that, one ends up burning out and eventually sacrifices their own health in order to succeed, and let me tell you from experience - it is not worth it. No matter the amount of money you make, it is not worth risking your own health over. You're not doing your clients and customers any favors when you're stuck in the hospital, no matter how many millions you have in your bank account. You won't feel content with your wealth when you work yourself sick and can't enjoy the quality of life that wealth affords you.

Find Your Mindset Ritual

Some businesses I worked with did a morning ritual to get into a positive mindset, such as setting goals for the day. This is a great technique for accomplishing tasks, one by one. What is even better is to learn a lifelong skill such as how to manage your emotional state when things don't go as planned and you must deal with a lot of objections before a sale happens.

Why, you ask? If you can manage your emotional state and mindset to be positive even when things get hard and still manage to be persistent, that is proof that you are ready to succeed with it.

Remember the story I told earlier where it took me two weeks before I got my first sale when I first started doing phone sales, selling Anthony Robbins tickets? If I would have given up after three days or a week, I would have gotten another secure 9 to 5 job and not become the person I am today, writing this book and sharing my experiences with you.

But, because I was persistent and did not give up, I ended up becoming one of the most successful sales consultants while I was selling other people's products and services on the phone. As a result, once one job finished, I got offered another one and so on. The longest I worked for a company was 5 Years which was 21st Century Education.

After that I returned to Switzerland, I worked for 2 other companies for about another 2 1/2 years before I made the decision to start up my own company to provide Businesses with my Expertise on how to provide better customer care and in doing so apply my Strategies so they can increase their Sales by 300%+ within their first 90 Days of working with me.

Sales Through Empathy

There are two things one needs to know about mindset: if you just try to do it from a logical standpoint without any emotions attached to what you are envision, it won't work. One needs to know that your mindset needs to connect to the emotions you are feeling with what you are envision to achieve or to feel.

Here is an example of what I mean. I strongly recommend practicing this exercise right now. I want you to close your eyes and just think or picture that you stand on mountain and you are looking down on to a beautiful little town, the sky is clear and the sun is shining with a little bit of wind blowing through your hair.

Now open your eyes again and observe what has changed in terms of your emotional state whilst thinking about it. Maybe it has shifted only slightly, but let's try it again, and this time let's go into it with more impact.

I want you to close your eyes and picture that you're standing on a mountain and you are looking down on at a beautiful little town, the sky is clear and the sun is shining with a little bit of wind blowing through your hair.

Keeping your eyes closed, I want you to remember a time when you felt happy, satisfied, and at peace. Visualize a moment when you felt pure bliss. Embrace those feelings within you, then turn those feelings up as you visualize yourself standing on that mountain, looking down on the little town whilst the sun is shining with the wind blowing through your hair.

Go one step further and let your thoughts pop up within you without trying to control them Let it happen for one minute. Soon you will feel blissful and happy. Then, open your eyes.

Now what did you observe? Wasn't that more powerful when we did it, this way then when we just used our logical mind to picture the mountain to stand on, I certainly believe so.

You can do this with any thoughts and emotions. The reason why I used this example is because when we make phone calls to make sales, or even to call a customer and resolve an issue, we need to be in a positive emotional state as well as in a positive mindset.

When you are in that state, nothing will stress you, and you will be in control of the conversation without stressing out or reacting to the customer's negative behavior towards you. Remember, you cannot solve issues or even sell anything when you are stressed and the customers will feel that on the phone when you are not in a positive frame of mind, this is why your mindset matters to make sales and to serve your customers better.

Chapter 6 - It's Not About the Outcome, It's About the Conversation

"Selling is not something you do to someone, it's something you do for someone."

When I trained other sales people and even business owners, I would often say, "It's not about the outcome, it's about the conversation you are holding with your customer."

All too often we end up focusing so much on what we want to sell to the customer and what we want, that we stop listening to what the customer is telling us from the get go.

I am sure you yourself might have had that experience when a sales person from a call center calls you up, reading out loud from a script to sell you insurance or something else, it must have felt forced, and all you wanted to do was get off the phone as soon as you could. Why? Because there is a disconnect when a sales person just reads out loud from a script without talking to the customer, it's like they are talking at you not with you, this is essentially a one-way conversation.

Then the managers of the call center or the business owners that lead their sales team are surprised when their conversion rate is only 1-3%. Use your common sense. You wouldn't want to be talked to any given time during the day when you have things to do, so why do you expect your customers to be okay with it?

This is what is wrong with cold calling but also with sales phone calls that are done to follow up with existing customers, there is no conversation happening, instead we just talk at them and hope they buy from us. What they end up doing is burn 99% of their existing bridges with their current customers and make it easy for their competition to take them from right underneath them when the customer is annoyed because of tacky sales, marketing, and survey calls.

Believe it or not, I had the best conversations when I just went with the flow and was listening to the customer, having a conversation with them instead at talking at them. Most of my sales came because of the high quality conversation I ended up having with them, not only because they ended up trusting me but also because we were able to have a good time on the phone holding a great conversation, having a laugh or even diving deep into personal matters that the customer felt right to share with me about him or herself because I connected with them on a deeper level, not just a superficial level where I told them about what I am here to sell, regardless if they were interested or not.

An Example of an Outcome Focused Pitch

Some customer service and even sales people are like bulldozers, they crash right into the customer without any regard for them. I once had a personal experience where I worked for Empowerment and they tried to outsource sales to India for Robert Kyosaki's "Rich Dad Poor Dad" Book and Seminar.

So, I get this phone call and an Indian man on the other end is telling me all about Robert Kyosaki, about the book and how great it is, half way through I tell him "I work for the company, I can get tickets myself if I want, so stop selling to me". Do you think he listened? No of course, not. He went right on and keep talking. I had to repeat myself three times and eventually I had to change my tone to the point where I was almost screaming into the phone to tell him to stop with the speech, because it was painfully obvious that he was reading from a script to sell those tickets.

Now, believe me that was very off putting and after that phone conversation ended, I hung up the phone, had a short laugh, and then told my supervisor "Saira" about what had just taken place. She had to laugh herself, shook her head and said to me, "They are trying to outsource the sales to India to save money".

My response to that was: "Well if they do that, in that fashion they will end up not only saving money but also lose more money than they would ever save doing that, so I don't think that is a smart move."

She then asked me, how did you enjoy the phone call with the Indian guy who tried to sell you the tickets to attend the Robert Kiyosaki Event?

I had to laugh and told her, "look that was one of the worst experiences I had having to listen to an aggressive, non-responsive sales person that is talking at me instead of talking with me. I wanted to hang up 10 seconds into it, but I didn't want to come across rude, however I had to tell him three times that I work for the company and he still didn't respond to what I was telling him, until I raised my voice for him to listen up, so I found that very much annoying." Besides if someone would talk to me that way like he did, they lost from the word go because I would not be interested to listen to them even if they were to sell me something that I would have an interest in because of their pushy approach, it is simply off putting.

That's why I say to you "It's not about the outcome, it's about the conversation you hold with your customers."

Make sure that whenever you have a conversation with someone that you hold it with them, not just talk at them, that is all I am going to say for now. Believe me, you will have it much easier when attempting to sell anything if you just have a conversation with someone rather than when you just talk at them.

Chapter 7 - Winning Someone's Trust is Hard Work, Losing it is Easy.

"Closing means always opening new relationships."

The reason I say "winning someone's trust is hard and losing it is easy" is because the competition today is much tougher than it used to be –especially with email marketing, online ads and big companies having the money to invest into TV ads to win over your hard-earned customers.

Here is the thing that I don't get: why are so many businesses focused on getting new customers and not looking after the existing ones?

Research has shown published by marketing metrics that existing customers are 60 - 70% more likely to buy again from you, if they are happy with your service and product. In comparison, new prospects that you approach with your product or service, to become a customer of yours, are only 5 - 20% likely to buy from you.

If I still haven't convinced you, the internet is awash with facts and studies that support these numbers. I have worked in the field of sales and customer service for more than 20 years, so I know that this data is true based on first-hand experience.

You can see more facts related to customer service on Help Scout: www.helpscout.net/75-customer-service-facts-quotes-statistics.

3 Things You Should Never Do to a Customer

Let's move on to how we can build a relationship with the customer, including 3 things you should never do to a customer. If you do one of those 3 things, it will only be a matter of time before you end up losing them to your competition. After all, "Winning a customer's trust is hard, losing it is easy".

1. Never ever argue with the customer over who is right, by trying to refer back to your policies or insisting on your point. Remember, the customer is always right, even when he is in the wrong. Instead of you arguing your point, see to it that you can sway your customer to agree with what you say and get them to a place where they are not emotionally charged, but rather in a place where a normal conversation can be held, then acknowledge what they went through, apologize and make it up to them in some way with a good gesture.

2. Prevention is always best, so from the beginning be transparent with your customers, don't have hidden fees, rules that are in small print no one can read or understand, and set clear verbal boundaries as well as to what they can expect working with you or buying your product. If you do that, you won't ever have to deal with customer complaints about being misled or that important information had been not shared with them.

Most companies, including startups, make agreements where they say that they deliver certain things but then in the end they don't, or they only do it partially because they cannot honor that kind of commitment.. So, now there is a conflict because they customer signed an agreement to get a service that he is not getting, of course he can complain about that, but the company includes small print within the agreement that they cannot be held liable for any changes that are made within the company's policy changes in terms of delivering the service the customer signed up for.

This is where it often gets messy, because the customer is within their rights to get the service they signed up for, but the company also has the right to do whatever they please, according to their terms and conditions that the customer agreed to.

Now, if I were the CEO of that company, I would make sure that, first of all, the agreement gets edited and outlined with exactly the service that the customer can expect to receive. Secondly, if that was not done right, I would side with the customer, make sure that the service that was promised to him will be delivered, regardless of the small print that is within the agreement. Because I understand the value of a good customer, and if one customer has a bad experience, he will tell at least ten people to never do business again with that company. If a customer is happy, he will for sure tell at least 3 people if not more about the great service he received from the company and how flexible they were to correct a mistake they made in the beginning.

3. If you provide any type of coaching, personal training and/or consulting, don't make your problems the customer's problems. By that I mean if the customer needs to reschedule his usual time with you and gives you anywhere between three to seven days' notice, even after it has been confirmed, then don't make a big fuss about it. The customer has every right even after the schedule has been confirmed to change his mind and ask for a re-schedule if he/she needs it. The customer is not interested in hearing about the stress you may be cause by having to shuffle other appointments around in order to accommodate them. My personal trainer that I am very fond of, did that just recently and it was a major turn off for me to stand there and justify myself to him. This was an exception to the rule for me as working out is very important but right now I have things in the pipeline for business that need to be taken care of and if the business people that I meet up with can only do it on

the day when I have personal training, then I need to re-schedule my training with him, it is as simple as that.

When you own and operate your own business, that is the downside of having to managing it. If you have a bigger business with more employees, that is still a downside which will never change. Sometimes, customers have to change things around because of their own business schedules. If they give you more than 24 hours to let you know, you should praise them, because believe me I had the experience where customers just didn't turn up or told me that they could not make it to a coaching session one hour before our agreed upon time.

So, don't give your customers a hard time about it just because it is an inconvenience to you. This is your job. You wanted to be self-employed or own a company that offers the customer a service, so take it on the chin and move forward.

Because if you do this, I promise you, the customers won't stick around for long. They might let it go one time but if you do this more than once, this kind of behavior is a major turn off for most customers.

The True Value of Customer Service

Again, and I'm going to repeat myself here but I want to really bring this point home. Instead of making your problem your customers problem, take a note from this next example.

Say a customer tells you 3 days ahead of the agreed appointment that they cannot meet because they have business meetings that came up which they simply must attend. Your response to that should be "Great, thank you so much for letting me know in advance, what days and times would be good for you to see me instead?" Or "Thanks for letting me know. Let me quickly check my schedule to see when we can meet up instead and suggest a couple of days and times that suit you".

The customer will appreciate your flexibility as well as not making a big deal out of it because most of the time the customer already feels bad for not being able to make the agreed time anyway, so there is no reason for you to make them feel even worse by patronizing him or complaining about said cancellation.

Now how can we assure that the customer is not losing trust? By keeping in touch with them, even outside of the appointments we have with the customer, we can make an effort to call them, see how they are doing and stay in touch with them. Once a customer is loyal to you, don't take the loyalty for granted, make an effort to always be great at communicating with them and show them that you care. You do all those things and avoid those three major mistakes that I just talked about, plus you keep in touch with your customers not only when there is something to sell but also to build a relationship with them, then you will have the customer for a lifetime, even when a better offer will come along, the customer will stay with you because they appreciate the value of your service.

According to an American Express survey, seven out of ten Americans said they were willing to spend more with companies they believe provide excellent customer service.

If you provide excellent customer service, your company will stand out from the competition, plain and simple. Unlike your competitor who may have mediocre customer service, you will be able to keep those satisfied customers long-term and they will refer plenty of new customers to your business.

Chapter 8 – What needs to happen to turn an Objection into a Sale

"Don't expect different results if your habits are the same."

While objections are usually the bane of every sales person, when you start to see an objection as just another opportunity, it can change everything.

There are many forms of objections when it comes to sales – all of which can be turned around and made into a conversion. From the buyer's perspective, an objection is really just a concern that they have about a specific part of the product or service you are selling. Maybe your price point is too high, maybe they see no practical use for what you're selling in their lives. Whatever the case may be, it's the salespersons job to smooth out objections.

The natural reaction of many sales people when they hear an objection is to tense up and prepare to be too down. What they should be doing is getting prepared to cross a bridge on the way to the sale.

The process of making a sale is a journey with many crossroads, only one of which is on objection. When an objection comes up during a sales pitch, what matters most is how you react to it. It is at that crucial part of a pitch when sales people must decide how far their relationship with their customers will go. Will you make a conversion and earn a customer for life, or will you let the sale go, and along with it, your customer?

As a sales person, you may be able to identify objections by listening and observing them, however, if you are preoccupied by what the customer is actually saying, you may be missing the things that they aren't saying. Listen carefully for things like changes in tone or an indication that something is wrong. Many times, customers can be too timid to ask questions about a product or service, or won't give you an exact reason for their objection. Customers often send mixed messages about what they do and do not want. While they may seem to say, "No, absolutely not", a salesperson should interpret that as "Don't proceed until you resolve this objection."

Types of Objections

There are many types of objections. Some are flatly stated, some are unstated, some are implied, and some need to be interpreted by the sales person. For every objection it is important to first identify the source of the objection before attempting to smooth it out and proceeding with a sales pitch.

Common objections include:

·   I have no need for your product or service at this time.

·   I have no ability to purchase or not enough money.

·   I don't trust in you as a person.

·   I have no hurry or urgency to act.

·   I have no interest in what you are selling because you haven't sufficiently captured their attention.

In order to make a conversion, a sales person must go beyond these common objections to discover the true objection. For example:

·   No need - "I'd like to use a product/service to enhance our situation, but what you are suggesting is not consistent with our specific needs."

·   No ability - "I want to go with you but I don't have the authority to OK this purchase" or "It extends my budget."

·   No trust - "The product/service seems good, but I'm concerned about you, your company, the quality of the product, or the likelihood of good service.

·   No hurry - "Your ideas are good but not exciting enough or valuable enough to get me to act now," or "Other items are more important to me right now."

·   No interest - "What I'm interested in and what you are proposing are not the same. So show me why I should listen to you."

In all of these examples, we can see how important it is to build trust with your client. Customers will be more willing to buy from someone who knows their individual needs and wants and how this product or service can specifically help them in their life. This is done by establishing familiarity and gathering information by asking as many questions as possible about the customer's particular circumstance.

Turning Objections to Sales

It's important that sales people ask for feedback during the entire process. This validates the customer and shows them that you are listening and genuinely concerned about their specific needs. Try to learn as much as possible about the customer during every single sales pitch.

So, the first step in the full process of turning an objection into a sale is first to relax. A customer will know if you tense up immediately after their objection.

Next, listen and intently observe both the verbal and nonverbal message of the prospect, both to what is being said and what is not being said.

Question their objection to make sure that you both understand the initial reason why they don't want to make a purchase. That way, you are both on the same page and there is no misunderstanding when you attempt to smooth out their concern.

Respond to the objection with genuine honesty, then, confirm the customer's answer to your response before proceeding with the sales pitch.

You will know if you made the correct or incorrect response to their objection based on verbal and nonverbal cues that immediately following your response. If your response was correct and on target, then the customer will become more engaged in the conversation. If not, they will persist with the same objection. At that point, a sales person must backtrack to get more clarity on what the customer is really objecting to. Listen for unstated objections as well as the ones that the customer verbally communicates. As such, being sensitive to the specific needs and wants of each customer is the best way to form your response to any objection.

The important consideration here is the word "overcome." If you overcome a person's objections, then you have simply beaten the objection down and he or she is the loser in the interplay between the two of you. Rather than "overcoming" an objection, it might be much more appropriate to simply "handle" the objection. Handling it means acknowledging the objection as genuine, showing the person that you are concerned, and taking the time to answer it appropriately rather than intimidating and making him or her feel silly through some smooth technique in which you "overcome" the objection through logic, psychology, and verbal prowess.

The important thing is to lower the tension between the two of you and maintain the trust bond. Selling today revolves around dealing with the prospect as a person, and as someone who has a need or a problem for which you can offer help. If you can do that, the sales process needn't be a battle. It doesn't have to be a situation with high levels of tension and stress. It can be a situation with a great deal of trust; and as trust goes up, so does your credibility and productivity. The prospect is more willing to cooperate with you and the bottom line is that you will increase your probability of making more and bigger sales.

Dario Cucci

Objection Resolution Techniques

Another important part to turning objections into sales is to never let the customer view you as an obnoxiously persistent sales person. Thus, any good sales person must learn how and when to resist, assist, and persist.

1. Resist - Resist the temptation to back off too early when faced with an objection. Hang in there. Also, resist the temptation to take the easy sale and not press on to fully solve the problem of the prospect.

2. Assist - Assist the customer in defining his or her real needs. Help him or her understand the basic problem that stimulated the objection. Don't just relate to the objection itself, but rather to the issue that really prompted the objection. Also, assist the person after the sale in gaining the maximum benefits from the product or service you have delivered. Follow up and follow through.

3. Persist: Persist in a way that shows that you genuinely are and you do want to be of service. When you use the techniques in the process we have described, you can persist without the intention of manipulating. You persist in a way that nonverbally conveys your concern and your sincerity. This strengthens that trust bond even further.

Here are a few key techniques which will help sales people handle objections as they arise and smooth them out on the journey to converting a non-customer into a customer:

1. Feel/Felt/Found. Example: "I understand how you feel" (I'm empathizing with you). "Many people have felt the same way" (That give you the feeling that you are not alone in all this). "However, they have found that . . ." (and you then present your solution). This could be offered in this way; "I understand your thinking. I thought the same thing when I first saw this product. However, I have found that . . ."

2. Convert to a question. When the customer makes a statement, many times it is difficult to answer the statement. However, you can convert the statement into a question that allows you to answer it more easily. Example: "I don't think I could use that product." Your response could be: "There is an important question I perceive in your statement and that is 'How can you gain maximum use from a product like this?'" Then you proceed to answer the question, not rebut the statement.

3. Echo technique. Sometimes you are faced with a response that really doesn't give you enough information. In this case you can reflect or echo it back to the prospect. The customer might say that the price is too high. Here, you can respond by saying, "Too high?" She or he will generally respond at that point by

giving you more feedback and information. From there, you can address the concern about price from his or her perspective.

4. Lowest common denominator. In this case you take an objection which has a big image in the prospect's mind and reduce it to a figure much easier to comprehend and handle. Example: "$300.00 is too much." Response: "$300.00 does seem like a large price tag until you consider that you will probably be using this 3,000 times a year, which means that your cost per usage is only 10 cents; a small price to pay for the increased convenience and profitability that comes from this product."

5. Boomerang technique. Think of a boomerang and what it does. Once thrown, it makes a wide arc and then comes immediately back to the individual who threw it. You do this same thing with a prospect's concern. He says to you, "I'm too busy right now to implement this new procedure." In this case you let his objection go past you and right back to him as the very reason he should buy now. For example: "The very fact that you are too busy to implement this feature right now is probably the main reason you should purchase it today." His response: "What?!" Your response: "The fact that you are too busy today means that you need more-than-ever the time-savings that will come to you as a result of using our product. So implementing this today will alleviate your problem of not

having enough time. It will actually give you more time to be more productive."

6. Change the base. In this case you take the basis upon which the customer is founding his or her response and change it so that he or she can see things in a different light. Example: The person says, "This won't accomplish the ABC process." Your response: "The main reason that you had inquired about this product was increased convenience. An added benefit, naturally, would be that it would accomplish the ABC process, but the point to bear in mind is that it does bring you the convenience that you require and, therefore, the ABC process should be secondary to any other considerations."

7. Compensation technique. Sometimes an objection is based on a very real product shortcoming that must be acknowledged. For example, a person might say, "This unit is too large for the space available." You could reply by saying, "I agree that it is larger than the space currently available, but the benefits of this product are so great that it would be unfair to deny yourself the benefits simply for the inconvenience of having to find a new space in which to put it." In this case, what you have done is say: "I agree that it is too big for that space, but the benefits of the product overpower that shortcoming, so let's go ahead with the purchase."

As you proceed down the crossroads of communication on your way to sales success, you are bound to encounter many objections. Knowing how to handle them makes all the difference between a sale and losing a customer.

Part Two Summary & Action Items

- The mindset in which you enter a phone call can often determine the flow of the conversation.

- Not all sales are created equal. The customer who feels pressured into a sale will never become a frequent buyer, but the customer who benefits from the product or service is much more likely to make another purchase.

- When you know the customer and their needs, it will be easier to find terms that you are both happy with.

- The reason a customer says "no" to something is because there are too many uncertain factors. Uncertainty comes from answering questions. Customers know what they want. For example, "If you were to give me a better price, I will do it." It's up to the salesperson to come up with terms that satisfy both parties.

- Remember, customer service isn't about dealing with a complaint, but serving your customer and seeing how you or your company can satisfy their needs.

Dario Cucci

Action Items:

1. Now that you know more about your customer, ask them direct questions about the product. What needs to happen in order to satisfy your customer?

   Implementation Tip: Come up with personalized solutions using your product in your customer's life. Example: "I bet these tickets would be a great gift for your wife. Didn't you mention your anniversary was coming up? I know a great baby sitter if you need one."

2. If a customer gives you an objection, do not get defensive. Instead, dig deeper.

   Implementation Tip: Try asking them to specify what they are objecting to and the reason behind it.

3. After addressing the objection, always ask your customer to buy.

   Implementation Tip: Try saying something like, "Are you ready to get started?" or "If I do this for you, will you stay with our company as a satisfied customer?"

PART THREE

Chapter 9 - Why Some CEOs Should Be Fired

"Sales go up and down. Service stays forever."

If you really want to know just how bad customer service can get, let me take you down the rabbit hole with my experience at Swisscom, Switzerland's biggest telecommunication company.

I was living in a Switzerland suburb just outside of a major city. There were these beautiful sprawling homes in every direction - but hardly any cell phone reception. Any time I would try to have a conference call, it sounded like someone was flushing a toilet. Obviously, this cell phone reception was hurting my business. In a place as densely populated as Switzerland, you would expect there to be decent cell phone reception.

I went into a local Swisscom store to speak with a customer representative so that they could solve my problem. What did they say?

They told me there was nothing they could do.

So, I asked to speak with someone from technical support, but they couldn't do that, either. The only way I was able to get someone on the phone was by telling them that I wasn't leaving until I talked to technical support.

After I explained that I wasn't able to get clear cell phone reception in my own home, these are the three options that the technical support representative provided me as potential solutions:

1.   Wait two years, which is when the company planned on upgrading their infrastructure in the area where I lived.

2.   Purchase what he basically described as a household cell phone tower for $500, plus installation and a monthly premium.

3.   Use Wi-Fi calling.

I weighed my options. Well, if that's all I have to make calls that don't sound like the person on the other end is gargling when I talk to them, then sign me up for Wi-Fi calling.

"Wi-Fi calling could fix the issue you're having with reception, but Wi-Fi calling isn't available for the type of phone you have."

Perfect.

The technical support representative proceeded to rattle off a short list of phones that would allow me to hear what the person on the other end was saying.

"So, let me get this straight", I then asked. "If I purchase a brand new phone – any of the new phones that you just listed – then I can use Wi-Fi calling where I live? And I can buy any of these phones from any store and use this feature?"

The answer was a confident "yes".

After following up on various technical support websites and forums to make sure that I could, in fact, use Wi-Fi calling to achieve clearer call quality, I made my selection from the list of phones that was presented to me – each in the $700 to $800 range. Naturally, I purchased one online at the best price I could find.

The phone arrived in the mail and I was overjoyed at the prospect of actually holding conversations with my clients. I powered on my new phone, signed into all of my accounts, personalized the settings, and everything else that you normally do when getting a new phone. But I couldn't figure out how to set up the Wi-Fi calling feature.

Again, I reached out to technical support for help. This time through the live chat on the company's website, which felt very much like I was speaking to a robot. He started by rephrasing my problem in the form of a question, then proceeded to read off of a script until I arrived at the conclusion that I would have was going to have to call customer support in order to talk to a live human being.

After calling in and reiterating my story three separate times while being transferred to three different departments, I finally reached someone in tech support who told me that the only way I could use Wi-Fi calling on my phone is if I purchased it in a Swisscom store.

For a moment, I thought I was stuck with two phones that served no other purpose than being very expensive doorstops. Was I mad? You better believe I was mad. But I was still focused on solving the problem and kept a cool head.

"Now you listen to me," I told the Swisscom technical support representative on the other end of the phone, "Everything in my home is packaged to work with Swisscom. I get a very large bill from your company every month, and every month I pay that bill on time. If you can't resolve this problem, I'm going to cancel my contract and take my business to your competitor. Then, I'll be forced to tell all of my friends and family what a terrible, disrespectful experience I had with Swisscom, at which point, I won't be the only customer you're losing. Now, maybe

I'll come back in two years from now when you straighten this situation out, or maybe I'll stick to paying your competitor for their services, I don't know. What I do know if that if this problem is not resolved in a timely manner that Swisscom will be losing quite a bit of money and customers."

After that, I asked to cancel my Swisscom contract, but their cancellations department had closed early that day. Instead, I hung up and wrote out a detailed complaint to their company.

What happened next? I got a call back within 24 hours of placing that complaint, apologizing and offering me a phone which did have access to Wi-Fi calling.

The point of my story is that some CEOs are so far removed from the everyday process of operating their businesses that they have no idea what's happening with their customers.

Chapter 10 - What Needs to Happen for Your Customers to Refer You

"Sell the problem you solve, not the product."

One of the biggest advantages of keeping your current customers satisfied instead of always chasing after new customers is that your current satisfied customers will bring the new customers to you. This is why good customer service is so important – when you do not impress, please, or satisfy your current customers, they will not recommend your business to their friends, family, and peers. Alternatively, good customer service only serves to grow your business.

Customer referrals really rock as a cost-effective way to gain new business and regain old customers. The magic of referrals is that they offer instant credibility.

Referrals come in a variety of different forms. If someone merely provides you a name and email address, that's low-grade referral. But if a customer actively talks up your product or service, sets up a meeting or brings the prospect in the door, that's a high quality referral, and very likely a customer who will end up becoming a brand loyalist who spends plenty of money on your products or services and eventually gives out even more customer referrals, thus expanding your business beyond what you thought possible.

Customer referrals are built on trusted relationships. Who better to refer you to a qualified prospect than your current clients who have received a great purchasing experience as well as measurable return on their investment directly from your products or services?

No one, because word of mouth is one of the most powerful ways to get new customers. So it would make sense to build a trusting relationship with your existing customers. This is why, in this chapter, we will address a few strategies of ways that you can increase your gross revenue - all through quality customer service.

Get Your Customers Talking

The best way to get your customers talking about you is to get them talking about you in front of you. By picking up the telephone, calling your customers, and asking them what they like or dislike about your products or services, you get the chance to connect with individual customers on a rare, one-on-one basis in addition to some priceless feedback on your actual products and services.

You might be pleasantly surprised to hear some authentic rave reviews. On the other hand, you may hear some items along the way you will want to improve upon, but that's all the better of a reason to make the call – you're getting real feedback from real customers, and whether you like it or not, take it in a way that will benefit your business.

As the customer shares with you what they like about you and your products or services, it's naturally going to make you feel good. This is nice, but the real value comes when you then ask the customer who if they have some names of other people who would benefit, too. Even better is if they are willing to introduce you to these people.

Because the question is such a direct one, calling your customers directly and speaking to them over the phone is just about the only way to ask them for referrals. A majority of customers will ignore an email with a similar message, but when you have a satisfied customer on the phone, you'll find that not a single one of them will end the conversation by hanging up on you, which as anyone who has done cold calls before know, is rare.

This process of calling customers and asking them what they like about you and what you sell does not have to be difficult. You should do it every 3 Months with every one of your customers to check in where they are at and how you can assist them even better with your Product/Services. Sadly, some salespeople only ask for referrals right after the customer has made their purchase. If you call your customers every year, though, you are able to use them as an on-going referral machine.

B2B Referrals

For those who work in a B2B environment, offer to them names of other people they might benefit from meeting. It's at this point you will have taken a call that began as a request for customer feedback and turned it into an opportunity to build each other's businesses. Swapping leads with other businesses is one of the easiest and most successful ways of not only retaining your customers, but satisfying them as well.

The Art and Science of Getting Referrals

Many businesses have turned the art of getting referrals into a science, calculating and tracking a Net Promoter Score (NPS). At its most basic, the NPS attempts to measure how likely it is that a customer would recommend a business, product or service to a friend or colleague.

"Promoters" are your most loyal and enthusiastic customers – the regulars who also refer others to help fuel your business growth. "Passives" are happy, but not enthusiastic and are easily attracted to a better deal elsewhere. "Detractors" are unhappy customers who can hurt your sales with negative word-of-mouth. The NPS is determined by taking the percentage of customers who are promoters and subtracting the percentage who are detractors. An equal amount of each gets you an NPS of zero.

Here are seven steps to getting better referrals and more of them:

1. Create a referral-generation plan: Referrals are not automatic. Some "just happen," but most occur because you do something to trigger it. Some business owners assume that a great product or terrific customer service will generate referrals by default. Not so. You have to learn to ask, and make sure

employees are on board as well. Most customers are open to being asked for referrals. Some even appreciate the opportunity to tell friends, family and associates about something good they've discovered.

Keep in mind that the worst time to ask for a referral is at the cash register or when you present a bill. Look for opportunities earlier or later in the process when customers are more receptive.

2.   **Provide support:** Don't ask customers to recommend you to others without offering them some backup. It can be as simple as a supply of your business cards, or a link to a special page on your website. Or it could be a brochure, your latest newsletter, or some other type of printed material that describes what you do and can reinforce the referral.

3.   Offer incentives: But incentives can be tricky. The type of incentive you offer must fit with the kind of business you run. It could be a discount, service credits, an upgrade, a free item or some other trigger that will entice clients to provide referrals. Don't be afraid to test offers to find out what works best. Communicate details of your referral program to your best customers through whatever means you have available, including a blog, newsletter, email or customer mailings. And be sure to thank customers when they make referrals.

4.   Ask for the right information: Getting a name and number isn't really a referral at all. It's just a lead. Use a referral form, checklist or web-based system to capture details that will make the referral more valuable. The best referrals are where a customer actually facilitates a meeting, visit or purchase by the referred person, in person, by email or otherwise. This makes the customer an active agent on your behalf.

5.   Target your most influential customers: Seek referrals first from your most influential customers, especially if your resources are limited. These might not actually be your best customers, but they are the people whose opinions would carry the most weight with others in your industry, community or customer base. By targeting these customers, you have a highly focused effort with a good chance to generate the highest quality referrals.

6.   Target related businesses: The health care profession is one of the most adept at fostering referrals between complementary disciplines – specialists, imaging services, physical therapists, medical equipment suppliers and others. Consider the same strategy yourself. Contact businesses that provide complementary services to your own and ask for referrals.

7.   Build your relationships: This takes time, but it's critical because many of your most influential customers won't provide referrals until you gain their complete trust. You'll want to treat each customer contact as if it's critical to your next referral. Through each sales, marketing or customer service "touch" you are building a foundation of trust that that will one day lead to a valuable referral.

As you continue to build up your customer referrals and expand your business, you'll be able to track which types of customers have the highest referral rate and who refers customers who end up spending the much.

Chapter 11 - Automation Killed our Communication

"Good service is good business."

Ever hear phrases like "The system won't let me do that" or "My department doesn't handle that"? These are just two examples of businesses with a failed customer service infrastructure.

When businesses begin to automate every process in their system, it doesn't leave room for custom solutions for individual customers. This is just one of the advantages that small business has over larger businesses who often automate things in order to make their sales process easier - but at what cost?

Surely, businesses who would rather automate than interact with customers one on one are taking a hit when it comes to customer retention, customer satisfaction, and even long term gross revenue. Slowly but surely, the way that we communicate with one another is changing, and some would argue that this change is not for the better. But, in the world of conversions (not sales), I'll show you how you can use the rampant automation employed by your competitors and turn it into a drastically higher customer satisfaction - and long term gross revenue - for you and your business.

Sadly, customers today have gotten used to being treated like second class citizens. In the digital age where social media dominates the lives of most, if not all, of your customers, authenticity is prized above all else. They are so used to interacting with people - even their closest friends and family members - that any form of authentic communication with another human being is often a pleasant surprise. For example, customers are pleasantly surprised when they find that they can actually reply to emails and speak with another human being.

The same is true for reaching out to customers on the phone. This is part of why establishing trust is such an important part of any sales pitch. Listening to your customer's needs and their particular circumstance is a highly effective sales tool. Sales people who interact with customers in person have even more of an advantage. Simple things like body language play a key role during in-person sales pitches and only help to further the customer-business bond.

Form a Bond with Your Customer

Businesses should think about their relationships with customers and clients that same that they would their relationships with their good friends. Some of the most successful sales people I have ever encountered were the most compassionate, understanding, and empathetic human beings I have ever encountered. What do all three of these assets have in common? They all stem from having exceptional communication skills.

While doing your market research on your competitors, it's important to not only see the best things that they do correctly (in the eyes of customers), but it's even more important to learn what customers don't like about certain aspects of the way they do business. If the other business uses automation in some capacity, you'll very likely be able to find some negative comments, critiques, or feedback from their current or previous customers.

When you find the negative feedback from customers of your competing business, then you have struck gold! This is exactly the area which you need to focus on fortifying in your own business. For example, when customers see that you have strong customer support and a very high customer satisfaction rating compared to your competitors, you won't have to fight to acquire new customers or struggle to keep the ones you already have, because they will love the purchasing experience you provide.

apter 12 – Why I Don't Like the Grant Cardone Approach

"Good salespeople are not born. They are trained."

I have seen him on YouTube videos and seen some of his tacky sales approaches, furthermore I heard also negative reviews about his tactics. However, what I don't like about him, is not his personality or anything like that, but his delivery on what sales should be like. I don't like that he thinks that mind manipulation to the extreme where people feel pressured to buy or act a certain way is okay to put out there.

Sure, there is the "Scare City Strategy", which works well because the customers require sometimes a bit of pressure to be motivated to make a decision to buy. On the other hand, I believe there can be such thing as too much of that, which is what Grant Cardone does and you see what I mean by just watching his videos, for me he comes across like a car salesman that is in overdrive, which I don't like. I believe that when you take things to the extreme and sell on people's fear it can come back to bite you in the butt. I experienced that firsthand when I used that strategy in the past.

The reason being is that if you as a customer are unsure and you only buy because it is great value and you like the product or service but you don't have the money, yet you want it, you will buy it and as soon as 1 hour, 1 day or even 1 week passes have buyer's remorse. Then, if those customers are outside the refund period you have to deal with them complaining that they been pushed into buying or they say you manipulated me into buying.

Neither one of those things are true but as mentioned before the customer is always right, and if their perception is that they were pushed into buying a product or service because of the sales person's approach then you need to fix that. What he does, is promote those Strategies online with his YouTube videos and his online programs and I feel it is his responsibility to show a different side of sales that is more sustainable than the "Scare City Strategy".

Transparency vs Trickery

When one is looked at as a role model and expert, one has the responsibility to make sure that the people that learn from him, know how to implement those strategies and when as well as when not to do them.

In general, "sales" has earned a very bad reputation because of people like Grant Cardone who utilize pushy and manipulative sales tactics. I have worked with people like that in the past, and every time without fail, when I approached them after they have spoken to a pushy sales person, they said to me "Thank God you are on the phone, it is so much nicer to talk to you than the other guy, I feel at ease with you and you know what, what you are offering sounds great, so how do we go about it?".

When the customer is ready to buy, they will ask how they can buy it, sometimes customers need more time if they are not ready to buy when you are ready to sell. However, you can inform and guide them along the way to get them to make a faster decision and still it does not need to come across as pushy.

What most sales people do wrong is they put too much emphasis on why the product or service or offer is special. For some customers that works, but for a lot of them it doesn't. We all have emotions, I am sure you heard the saying "That customers buy because of the emotion they felt when they looked at a product or imagine what the service could do for them". So, why not engage the conversation on a level with the customer where they get emotionally involved rather than just logical?

If you know the sales relationship strategy that I use, you should easily be able to do just that and guess what, when you know how to create urgency in the customer that you are talking to, more often than not, they will buy from you.

Chapter 13 - Why a Sales Script will Limit Your Sales

"One customer taken care of could be more valuable than $10,000 worth of advertising."

I am sure that you've gotten this phone call more than a handful of times: "Hi this is James from Nobody Company. Is this Mr. Cucci? Yes. It is? Okay, great, I just called because…"

One minute later, without him ever asking me a single question, the telemarketer will say something along the lines of, "So, how does that sound to you?"

Most of the time, I will interrupt them in the middle of their spiel and say that I am not interested. If they get to the end, and even if I were to be slightly interested, I am put off by that whole approach so much that I end up telling them I am not interested.

I am sure you have had experiences like this, too. If it's not obvious yet, let me spell it out for you: "SCRIPTS DO NOT WORK!"

I hope that I've made that clear. I've worked with scripts when I had to in the past, but believe me, more often than not, I changed them around or ended up not using them entirely because the way I talked to the customer sold more products and services. When my managers saw that I was going off-script, they didn't care because my sales numbers were still higher than anyone else. Despite the fact that they saw my method of selling brought in more money on a consistent basis, everyone else still stuck to a sales script.

Know the Framework

I normally teach my clients to stick to a simple framework – not a script. They learn to be authentic over the phone whilst implementing that framework and how to hold a conversation that leads to a sale.

If I am working with a company on customer retention or customer care, I do the same thing. My clients always learn the framework much quicker than the time it takes to memorize a script - and they get better results.

When I trained the acquisition and sales team at 21st Century Education, I used a similar framework on how to hold a conversation with the leads in order to get new customers and even to sell more products to existing customers.

Within a period of one week, they were able to do that without me having to control every word they said on the phone. Within two weeks, we increased the appointment setting for the sales people by over 300%. In that same two weeks, the sales department increased sales by an average of 300%. While all of this was going on, every individual within the company structure was able to stay true to himself without having to follow strict guidelines to what can be mentioned on the phone and what can't.

This is the reason why this particular method works so well: every human being has an internal instinct. They know when they are being lied to and they know when someone is faking it. This same instinct allows them to sense when the other person at the other end of the phone is reading from a script in order to simply make a sale. People buy from people they trust, and trust can't be established by reading from a script.

So, whenever someone hands you a script in order to sell products or services over the phone, toss it in the garbage and give me a call instead.

Part Three Summary & Action Items

- Never read off of a sales script! Having an authentic conversation with your customer will be much more successful.

- Be flexible and willing to create personalized solutions and deals for each individual customer.

- All customers are unique and require a unique approach before they convert into loyal customers.

- Remember the wise, old adage, "The customer is always right!"

Action Items:

1. Be more transparent with your customers in order to build trust.

   Implementation Tip: Tell them exactly what product or service you are offering, how much it costs, and how it can help them.

2. Refuse to resort to sales psychology, manipulation, and other underhanded sales strategies.

Implementation Tip: Keep your conversation honest, fair and always remain professional.

3. When you make a promise to your customer, always keep that promise – at any cost.

   Implementation Tip: If you're working with a lot of different customers, it's a good idea to keep a spread sheet where you can make a note that you promised them a certain thing. If you need to deliver what you promised at a later date, be sure to add that to your calendar.

4. Don't revert to the terms and conditions on your products as a reason that you can't meet your customer's demands. Instead, leave room for personalized solutions.

   Implementation Tip: Offer each and every customer a customized solution to their problems. This will cement your relationship and they will be more likely to become a bran loyalist.

5. Review your policies, terms and conditions. Get them re-written so that they are more transparent. Your customers should know exactly what they are getting and what they aren't.

Implementation Tip: For example, instead of writing your terms in technical or legal language, write them in common, conversational English.

PART FOUR

Chapter 14 - The Myths of Sales and Customer Service

"Your customers don't care how much you know until they know how much you care."

Every business needs to start with a certain amount of new customers in order to make a profit, this much is true, however, where most businesses go wrong is that they focus far too much and end up spending far too many of their resources on acquiring new customers when they can hardly fulfill the needs of their existing customers.

Companies of all sizes often get caught up in "keeping their eye on the prize", and end up hiring an entire task force whose sole job is new customer acquisition. This obsession with "company growth" actually proves detrimental to most corporations and small businesses in the long run.

However, for existing and established businesses, their most predictable and reliable source of revenue is something that they already have. It's not something that they need to search very hard for and it's certainly not something that they need to spend billions of dollars in marketing in order to retain. That's right – I'm talking about their existing customers.

Think about it – customers who have previously spent money on your products or services are the best candidates to spend more on your business. This is because you don't need to spend the time explaining the product or service to them and they are already familiar with your company. So, by prioritizing customer service instead of actively seeking out new customers, businesses are able to double or even triple their revenue.

Let's look at some common misconceptions when it comes to prioritizing customer service while putting customer acquisition on the backburner.

Customer Service Myth #1

Our previous customers already spent money on our products or services, therefore, they will not spend any more money on our business.

Myth Buster:

This is perhaps the most common misconception when it comes to customer services and marketing. You can almost hear the flaw in logic of this statement. Here is why this is wrong – and will end up costing companies a lot of money if they follow this train of thought.

There are few exceptions that apply to this statement. If you sell something that has a one-time use – something that your customers will only purchase once and never again – then they might not spend money on your business again.

First of all, I don't recommend anyone own this type of business. You should always be selling some sort of supportive accessories as an offshoot of your main product or service. Ask yourself, "What else do customers who spend money on my product/service spend money on?"

If it's something that you cannot provide yourself, there is most likely an affiliate website where you can become a partner and start making affiliate sales. We'll look at how you can make money on affiliate sales in more detail later in this book.

Another approach to increasing your sales and revenue if you sell a one-off product that has little repeat business is, if they had a great customer service experience and you provided a pleasant buying experience all of the way through, they will be extremely likely to recommend your product or services to a friend or colleague. Thus, by providing an awesome buying experience from the very beginning to the end (followed by awesome post-purchase customer service, of course), you will be essentially doubling your revenue from a single customer after they recommend new paying clients.

Easier said than done. Businesses who offer some kind of referral program in which they reward their previous customers for recommending your products/services to their friends, family or business colleagues are known to earn up to five times more than companies who don't have a referral program.

Here is a short list of some successful companies who have customer referral programs and what they offer previous customers as a reward for bringing in new clients. Use this list to get an idea as to what incentives you should offer your customers:

1.   Dropbox – Refer a friend to Dropbox and they hook you up with more storage space than you know what to do with.

2.   Hulu – This paid video stream service offers two weeks of their service for free with every referral.

3. Fiverr – The user-operated hodgepodge of services starting at five dollars will pay you ten dollars in credit when you refer a new customer.

4.   Many gyms give a free month to their customers for bringing in referrals.

5.   My personal trainer gives me a free hour training session when I refer him a new customer. Since he charges two hundred dollars per hour, this is a great value for clients such as myself.

Here are the best ways to go about setting up an effective referral program that will get you new customers and double your gross revenue in a matter of weeks:

1.   Make it easy for your previous customers to refer new customers

2.   Make sure that your previous customers are well aware that you offer a referral program and make sure that they know

exactly what they will receive by referring a new customer to you.

3.   Be transparent with your terms in regards to the Referral Program

4.   Don't stop at just one referral, have a Referral Program that allows them to benefit from referring more than just one or two of their Friends.

5.   Don't be stingy! If someone is bringing you new customers, each and every one of those referrals have the potential to become loyal to your brand and earn your company THOUSANDS OF DOLLARS (depending on the price of your products/services) over the course of a LIFETIME!

Most companies have an automated referral program, but they lack the customer service aspect of it. I know that a combination of automation with the proper customer care communication strategy in place, can not only win you new referrals but also make you additional sales when done the right way. I teach my clients exactly that when I meet with them, on how to hold these kinds of conversations to get new referrals from their existing customers over the phone whilst also making them aware of what else they might need from us by hold a proper in depth conversation with them.

You don't want to do what everyone else does because that will be boring. You will not stand out from your competitors. You want the customers to rave about your quality customer care service and consultants that deal with them. It will cause a positive after effect when your customers speak about your business. They will not only promote you in the public eye and on social media, but they will mention you to their friends, colleagues and families. They will tell them how great the experience of being one of your customers is because of the conversations you have with them.

We all know the story of Facebook. Facebook is a perfect example of this; they started with a few people at first, every single one of those people talked about it and told their friends, and as a result, it grew like wildfire without them having to spend a dime on advertising.

You want that for your business; you want the positive experiences the customers have with you to spread like a wildfire.

Customer Service Myth #2

It's easier to sell low priced items than high priced services.

Myth Buster:

Incorrect. I sold high end programs at times much faster than when I had to sell something that was cheap. It all comes down to the way you hold the conversations with your customers and get them to see the value for them when they make their purchase through you. Since customers are more comfortable in buying things from people they trust, if you don't come across as confident and knowledgeable about the product you are selling, the customer won't trust you and therefore will not buy from you. This is something I've seen happen time and time again, no matter the product or service.

Customer Service Myth #3

The best way to increase sales revenue is with new customers.

Myth Buster:

This is a myth that ends up costing many companies of all sizes a lot of money. What would you rather have? 100,000 one-time customers that just bought your product or service because of a special offer, or 50,000 customers that keep coming back to buy more from you?

Naturally, getting repeat sales from existing customers provides only long term revenue for businesses. It also saves them a ton of dough on marketing campaigns and acquisitions. Those customers will also be the ones that refer new customers to you by sharing their positive purchasing experience with their friends, family, and on social media.

On the other hand, those other many customers who only made one purchase from you in order to get the special deal, but then didn't return to place another purchase because of the bad customer support they experienced or the lack of customer care, they will not only remember that experience, but they will bring their business your competition and end up giving you bad reviews. In the long run, all of these things combined can add up, costing a business thousands, or even millions of dollars.

Customer Service Myth #4

One needs a lot of cash for advertising and marketing in order to win new customers and build up a business.

Myth Buster.

Big corporations want the small business owners to believe that marketing and advertising is some enormous task that can only be successfully done with an equally enormous budget. This is an intimidation tactic used by larger corporations in order to make small business owners believe that competing with them in the same market is virtually impossible. However, the truth is that in the age of digital advertising, nothing could be further from the truth.

Pay-Per-Click ad publishers, like Google AdWords and Facebook, make acquiring new customers simple and affordable. But the fact is, it is not about how many new customers that you get, but how you serve them. Small businesses have the advantage of being able to easily implement changes to their structure in order to accommodate the needs of their customers and improve their customer service to serve their customers better than the big corporations can. They have way too many ridiculous structural and administrative rules on how to deal with the customer to be able to just apply the changes required to serve their customers better and increase sales. As a small business you don't need a big advertising budget to make more sales; just start to improve your communication skill and implement a customer sales relationship strategy within your business to get more repeat sales and more new referrals, as a result you will be able to build momentum within your business without having to spend a dime or very little on advertising.

Chapter 15 - Real Talk Will Make You Win Real Customers

"Quality is remembered long after price is forgotten."

Creating customers who are loyal to your brand is the secret to a successful business. Giant corporations like Pepsi and Wal-Mart use this strategy, as do relatively unknown small businesses who are developing their own unique and quirky brand from the ground up.

The average cost of acquiring a new customer is five to ten times as much as it costs in marketing in order to get a previous customer to make another purchase. This is because you are focusing all of your time and resources on influencing someone who has already spent money on your products or service and convincing them to make a second (or third, or fourth, or tenth!) purchase.

But don't go and fire your sales people just yet – you can just as easily come up with a new sales strategy that focuses on your existing customers. Let's consider for a moment what the difference is between your existing customers and your potential new customers.

Building Relationships with New Customers

First, what do you need to spend time on in order to make a sale with a new customer?

1.   New customers need each product/service you offer explained to them, often in great detail.

2.   New customers need to understand the value of your products or services for each price point.

3.   New customers need to be made comfortable with your brand and often they need to learn about your history.

4.   You must build up a certain level of trust with your new customers before they spend money with your company.

Now let's revisit those points with your previous or existing customers:

1.   Your existing customers are already familiar with your products and services.

2.   Your existing customers are already familiar with your price points.

3.   Existing customers are already comfortable with your brand and they often know about your history.

4.   Existing customers have established a certain level of trust in your company – enough to make a purchase decision.

This is just a short list summarizing some of the basic difference in marketing to new customers versus existing customers. Obviously, there are many more difference than those listed here, but we can already see how much time and energy we save ourselves by focusing our marketing efforts on existing customers rather than acquiring new customers.

So, in addition to saving you time by focusing on existing customers rather than educating new customers – THEN convincing them of the value of what you sell, you are essentially making more money over a longer period of time.

The transaction based value of customers is an archaic one. This is what drives the "new customer acquisition" marketing mentality. This was the way that most businesses operated in the 50's and 60's during the peak industrial growth in America, when companies like General Electric were trying to sell a television set to every household in the country, however, this is no longer the case.

Chances are, you aren't selling televisions. You aren't even selling a new invention – you're likely selling something that is available at any number of stores. So, why would customers choose your product or services compared to any other place

127

where they can spend their money to purchase basically the same thing?

The answer? Brand loyalty. People fall in love with brands. They love your story, your message, they love the way that you package your products or the way that you carry out your services. This creates brand loyalists and repeat buyers. Your goal as a business should be to turn every customer into someone who is loyal to your brand.

The best example of this is Apple. "Apple People" are known to buy Apple products, regardless of the quality or specifications of their products. They trust the brand. The brand has never done them wrong. And the thing about hardcore brand loyalists, like "Apple people" is that Apple could come out with a new iPhone that has less than half of the capabilities as their competitor's new product – and Apple would still make a fortune selling it.

In the long run, this saves Apple billions of dollars on marketing each and every year because they have guaranteed sales stored away via their brand loyalists. This also creates an international free marketing campaign for Apple, because Apple's brand loyalists are out there telling their friends, family, and often even strangers how great the latest Apple product is.

Lifetime Customers & Brand Loyalists

Creating lifetime customers should be the goal of each and every business. This is easy to do once you start thinking from the mindset of your customers.

On the road to creating a brand that your customers love, you should create an ideal customer.

We mentioned earlier in this book that your business should never follow the "one and done" architecture of selling only one product. You should always be able to upsell something that your customers *need.* Find out what they are buying, then, offer that. Create a package deal if you have to. This will convince your customers that they are getting even more value for their purchase. They will also be concerned about the price, because the convenience of purchasing everything they need all at once is a valuable transaction indeed.

Chapter 16 - The Importance of Powerful Email Marketing

"Customer Service is worthless. Customer loyalty is priceless."

When it comes to customer service, be sure to follow up with your existing customers!

In order to keep in touch with your customers, most businesses set up an auto-responder sequence of emails. This can be done though any number of email marketing service providers such as Mailchimp (for beginners), Aweber (intermediate), or Infusionsoft (for experts).

By the way, just because I have listed Infusionsoft as an "expert" email marketing tool, that doesn't mean it's the most effective, or the right one for you. Infusionsoft has a notoriously large learning curve for new users, whereas Mailchimp is extremely user friendly, so if you are new to the world of email marketing, I recommend starting there and then progressing to the next tool once you become more familiar with how email marketing works.

Alternatively – simply hire a professional to take care of all of this for you!

The reason automating your email marketing is so important when it comes to engaging and selling to your existing customers is because it will allow you to stay in contact with each and every customer while freeing up the time it would take to manually email every customer after every purchase they make.

From the moment you make your first sale, your automated email sequence should take your customer on a journey. One that not only tells the story of your brand, but it should offer valuable information, coupons and even free products along the way in order to keep your customer engaged. Otherwise, when your customers cease to open your emails – you've lost them! And at the point it can take just as much work to get your previous customers back on your side as it does to acquire new customers.

Of course, email automation is no substitution for authentic human connection. Always encourage your customers to reach out to you with any of their comments, questions, and especially their complaints. Addressing these issues is just one way to humanize your business and show that you care about individual customers.

When you own a physical business and you get to see your customers in person you are ten times more effective because it is that much easier to build and nurture relationships with your customers.

A recent study determined that customers based their decision of where to shop and which stores they intended to spend their money on a number of factors, ranging from location and the proximity of the store adjacent to the location of their home, the current deals and promotions the store was having, the selection of the store's products in terms of quality, etc. Unsurprisingly, the biggest contributor to why customers decided to shop at a specific store was based on their relationships with people who worked at the store. This included knowing a friend, neighbor or family member who worked at the store, but also simply having a rapport with a store clerk or store manager.

What this means is that customers who make small talk with store employees are the most likely candidates to be loyal to a brand.

This determines not just which chain or franchise customers prefer to shop at, but the specific location of a particular store.

As we can see, there is a lot that can be gained by simply engaging your customers more. Using this same concept, wouldn't it be more effective for large business owners and franchise operators to train their employees in the art of customer engagement as a method of upselling?

If massive companies such as McDonalds and Wal-Mart focused on training their employees to simply be friendlier with customers instead of which buttons they need to push on the cash register, how much on an increase do you think they would see in gross revenue every year?

Most companies who make the shift from traditional marketing tactics to customer service centric "marketing" see no less than a 300% increase in revenue within their first year. For companies like McDonalds and Wal-Mart – which many people I know actively avoid because of the dismal customer service – that change would have a massive impact. Not just on their revenue, but in the way that customers see their brand.

In the words of a friend of mine, who is also a business owner, "I actively avoid going to places like McDonalds and Wal-Mart if I can. I would never willingly choose to patronize either of those places because of the sad way that their employees go about work. You can hear the apathy in their voice and see it in their body language and it's clear that either their employers mistreat them or they simply hate their jobs. When you leave a place like that, that apathy has a tendency to follow me around. I actually leave those stores in a sadder state than when I arrived."

That's the opinion of one person, who also happens to be a friend and client of mine. He understands the importance of employees at all levels of a business connecting and interacting with

Do you agree with his statement above?

Send me a Tweet @DarioCucci and let me know what you think – I would love to hear your opinion.

Chapter 17 - The Secret to Consistently Increasing Your Revenue

There is only one way which will allow you to see consistently increasing revenue and create an income for yourself that only grows and grows, and that is through keeping track of your analytics and proper maintenance of your company's infrastructure.

Setting up analytics for your website, your social media, and just about anywhere you interact with customers will allow you to refine your sales tactics and constantly improve your marketing. Only through self-analysis can you constantly hone your customer service, improve upon what is working, and change what isn't.

By now, you probably have a sales pitch which works pretty well for you. Maybe sometimes it isn't as effective as other times and you chock this up to it being the fault of the individual client, right?

Wrong.

Part of creating an ever increasing revenue stream involves mastering not just your sales pitch, but timing your sales pitch just right. This is where your analytics come into play.

Take the role of an internet marketer, for example. They have access to hard data that tells them the exact times and dates when they are making the most sales. They can see all of the factors that contribute to each sell and are therefore able to refine their digital sales process. This is the same approach that any salesperson should take in order to constantly increase their sales while building relationships with customers.

One advantage that a person who sells products or services over phone has over an internet marketer is that the salesperson who is actually speaking to their customer can hear the emotion in their voice. They can hear all of the little annoyances, excitement, disinterest, and conviction. Likewise, someone who sells in person has the advantage of being able to see a customer's expressions and body language.

Now, with every customer you interact with, whether it results in a sale or not, I want you to make a mental note of every factor which you believe may have contributed to the customer making their decision to buy or not buy. If a person is having a bad day, well, there is a reason behind that. They may not presently be in the mood to buy from you, but when you focus on building relationships as the end goal – not the sale – that same person will almost always change their mind. After all, every day can't be a bad day.

When you think analytically and communicate openly, you'll find that sales start to come freely and frequently.

That's not to say that selling products and services over the internet doesn't have its own advantages when it comes to customer relationship building.

Case Study

Here is a case study from one of my students which illustrates exactly how to take the strategies I teach and apply them to your own business:

"I launched my first FREE online e-course on the 18 August 2016, '7 Key Steps to Get Your Expenses Done in less than 10 mins a day'. On the following day, I had put a limited offer low-priced e-product for sale at a mere £3.00. In less than 24 hours, I made my first sale of £3.00. Although it was only £3.00, it did feel like a win! I was really thrilled and hopeful that the money will start flowing in.

Then, nothing happened.

The days went by and I continued developing my business. I was actively participating in groups on social media. But I was not making any sale. Within 2 weeks of the e-course launch, on the 31 August 2016, Dario Cucci connected to me on one Facebook group. Then we had a Skype call.

I explained my situation to him, how I was struggling to make sales. I had only just started this business since March 2016 and I had spent many hours and money already, building it up. Now I needed to get clients.

Dario was able to understand my situation. He went on to give me advice on communications strategy and the importance of customer service. He had various ideas on price strategy and he showed me how to implement a sales strategy to get more clients.

From that initial call, Dario had already shown me various new ways of creating products packages and he encouraged me to create a £77.00 products package and launch it to my existing leads. On the 4 September 2016, I sent my first campaign promoting the £77.00 offer. I kept promoting and I waited.

I had my first coaching session with Dario on the 6 September 2016. Of course we discussed about the £77.00 offer and Dario showed me how to improve the existing campaign. He redesigned it and gave me further actions plans to implement on sales strategy. I was more than keen to give it a try as I needed to get more clients. I took action on his sales strategy and it works!

On the 8 September 2016, I made my first £77.00 sale! Rebecca Marsden, the Puppy Owner Specialist took up the offer of £77.00 after joining the Finance For Creative People and implementing the '7 Key Steps to Get Your Expenses Done in less than 10 mins a day'.

The sale that I made took place 4 days after the launch of the £77.00 offer. If you look at the percentage change, this is a 2,466.67% increase in sales from my starting £3.00 sale...

I would highly recommend Dario Cucci as a mentor, a coach, a communications optimization expert, and sales trainer. He has a real insight into sales and communications and if you implement his communications strategies in your own business, you will learn how to improve customer service and increase your sales in order to make more profits."

Melanie Lam, Founder of "Finance For Creative People" (https://m.facebook.com/financeforcreativepeople/)

Feel Free to Join Finance for Creative People programs. The "7 Key Steps to Get Your Expenses Done in Less than 10 Mins a Day" eCourse is FREE exclusively to those who purchased this book here:

https://financeforcreativepeople.leadpages.co/finance-for-creative-people/.

Melanie also has a wonderful eCourse, "Start Your Journey To Financial Freedom - Get Out Of Debt", also available for free exclusively to those who purchased this book here: https://financeforcreativepeople.leadpages.co/start-your-journey-to-financial-freedom-get-out-of-debt.

Part Four Summary & Action Items

- Be warry of customer service myths and people spreading misinformation. Stick to what you know works.
- Complete transparency throughout the sale is one of the major keys to building customer relationships.
- Start taking mental notes on what factors contribute to each customer making a decision to buy or not to buy.
- Think analytically; communicate openly.

Action Items

1. The last action you need to take in order to increase your sales and solidify your relationships with customers is to enroll in my free 30-minute Discovery Session. This is my free gift to you to show my appreciation for reading this book, normally valued at $250. If you're serious about increasing sales and customer service, enroll in your free Discovery Session at www.DarioCucci.com.

2. Finally, if you enjoyed reading this book and found the strategies helpful, please take the next 90 seconds to write an honest review of this book so that others may also benefit from its contents. Thank you.

About Dario Cucci

With over 20 years of working in sales and customer service, Dario Cucci now shares his experience and knowledge with people and businesses in order to help them build better sales through better relationships with customers. Keeping a customer happy and loyal is much less costly than finding a new one.

In his program, Dario teaches a simple, efficient, and practical way to build a better and more sustainable sale. He is committed to building true customer care and helping companies build relationships with their customers. The result is mutually satisfying: lifelong loyalty in customers and long-term sales for companies.

Dario first learned how to sell in his twenties when he made his living from 100% commission-based selling with Anthony Robbins Events. Over the next 15 years, he has developed and refined his own relationship sales system that teaches how to build relationships that lead to sales and long-term loyalty.

Today, Dario travels the world speaking at seminars and conferences where he helps people and businesses increase their sales by up to 300%, although his private coaching students often see better results in less than 90 days.

To show his appreciation for everyone who purchased this book, Dario Cucci is giving away a free 30-minute Discovery Session, valued at $250. Discover how you can increase your sales today at www.DarioCucci.com.

Made in the USA
Columbia, SC
22 April 2018